Fatal Flaws of Employee Wellness Programs

How to Create a Corporate Wellness Strategy that Works!

Alison Brehme

Copyright © 2019

All rights reserved.

ISBN-13: 9781077916098

DEDICATION

To my parents, there are no words to fully express how grateful I am to you both for your continual love and support. I love you both!

CONTENTS

Foreword	1
Introduction	5
Why Care About Corporate Wellness?	15
How Does a Company's Culture Relate to Corporate Wellness?	25
What Four Strategies Are Needed for Corporate Wellness?	31
What's Your Purpose and Vision? Defining Common Sense Goals and Objectives	33
A Brutally Honest Assessment of Your Company	39
Create and Implement a Data-Based Strategy	53
Tracking Your Progress: Show Me The Numbers	71
Wrap Up	83
About the Author	87
Resources	89

ACKNOWLEDGMENTS

First and foremost, I'm grateful to God. He gave me the inspiration for this book and the courage to take a running leap into a different world. It wasn't easy. It was scary, but I am glad I listened to that still-small voice inside. If you have an idea that you can't seem to shake, I want to encourage you today to take that leap of faith. It's worth it!

This book is dedicated to my parents. Thank you for showing me the value of hard work and to never give up on my dreams. Your encouragement, love, prayers and support are what kept me going especially in those moments of uncertainty. I'm truly blessed to have you both!

To Pedram Shojai, thank you for being a guiding light and true champion of wellness. I've learned a lot from you over the years and I am forever grateful for the opportunity to work as a lead coach with you training students at Well.org's Corporate Wellness Academy.

To Cynthia Pasquella-Garcia, Maria Andros, Camden Hoch, Salt Freedom, Jodie Wallace and Linda Floyd for your encouragement, guidance and support as I pursue my business dreams and goals. The input from each of you has been invaluable and I am beyond blessed to have known and worked with each of you.

I'm grateful to all the fabulous companies, coworkers and colleagues I have worked with over the years. No company is perfect, yet I know I learned so many valuable lessons. It truly was an honor and privilege!

I feel like the music at the Oscars is going to start playing at any moment...

To wrap up, thank you to all my family and friends both near and far. I'm truly blessed to have you all in my life.

And a special shout out to Kim with NewFrontierBooks.com who helped me bring this to life!

FOREWORD

There's a health crisis in the western world that is sliding faster than we've been able to fix it. People are suffering from chronic lifestyle diseases and are gaining weight. They're losing sleep, ailing with pain, and not getting much better with traditional care.

We know there's an issue and tell people they should "eat better" or "get some exercise". We may blame it on laziness, lack of discipline, a broken healthcare system, or Washington but the facts remain the same: we're sliding.

This comes at an enormous cost to society. People die. Mothers and fathers are lost. Workers show up and pretend to stay busy at the job. Costs go up and jobs are cut. Accidents happen and lives are changed forever.

These are real occurrences happening every day and companies are struggling to find solutions. They need a healthy workforce. They desire happy, motivated, positive people who show up and add value in the career they're involved in. What they get oftentimes is migraine headaches, back pain, stress, anxiety, and emotional upheavals at work.

Enter the new era of Corporate Wellness.

We can no longer afford to tell people to do "that health thing" at home and come to work ready to sit still for 8 hours a day. We can't stock company break rooms with sugar and coffee and wonder why diabetes is on the rise. The fact is, most Americans spend over an hour a day on the road. That means with eight hours of sleep, one hour on the road, and eight hours of work, there are seven hours remaining to live life. That includes meals, showers, shopping for groceries, more driving, and hopefully some time with the family. Time for the gym is hard to find in all of this.

We can no longer ask people to stay stagnant for 8 hours a day and expect them to be healthy.

Still water breeds poison.

People need to move and get fresh air. They need to stretch and drink more water. That seems like a "cost" and something they need to do after work hours but we've come to learn that these practices are critical to the health, wellbeing, and happiness of human beings. These humans make up our companies and support the economy. They are the single units that make up the teams that make the world go. Keeping people moving, eating right, taking personal time to be happy, and resting when tired just makes sense…but how do we do it?

Enter Alison Brehme.

She's on the cutting edge of where the true benefits of corporate wellness can be realized. The key is to charge the workforce with fun and engaging activities that get them involved while simultaneously tracking and monitoring progress so the CFO sees positive returns on investment.

It's not easy but it's the only game in town.

We need to help people and track the results in a way that makes any wellness program a true win/win/win. The employee wins, the companies wins, and the consultant also wins. This means understanding how to structure programs, how to track them, and how to charge reasonable fees.

Alison is one of the best at this. Her work is inspiring and has changed many lives. She's a pioneer in the field and is a sane voice of reason in an industry riddled with pretenders and slick salespeople.

You are in the right place. Enjoy the pages of this book and absorb everything. It'll help you understand how to do corporate wellness the right way. That way we can actually help people and resolve the healthcare crisis where people spend a full third of their lives...at work.

Pedram Shojai, OMD
NYT Best Selling Author of The Urban Monk, Rise and Shine, and The Art of Stopping Time
Producer of the films: Vitality, Origins, and Prosperity
Founder of Well.Org

INTRODUCTION

Corporate wellness does not work. There. I said it. Maybe that's not something you expect a certified consultant to say, but I believe it's the truth. Why? Because most corporate wellness programs have one or more fatal flaws:

1. True leadership is missing. The program development is often rushed – something that is checked off a to-do list instead of thoughtfully incorporated into the company's culture.
2. There is no clear vision or strategy when the program is designed.
3. The program's execution does not match its goals.
4. Employees are not involved in the process.
5. Results are not tracked, or the focus is on the wrong key performance indicators (KPIs).

Your employees are the heart of your business, and they should be the focus of your corporate wellness program as well. They are, after all, your best asset.

But employees today are stretched thin, facing pressures from every side. Obviously, they have families, friends, and lives outside of work. They want to "have it all," yet often feel forced to choose between peace at home and peace at work. With stress on the rise, with healthcare costs climbing, with loss of productivity and profits because of sick employees – at what point do we stop?

I'm pumping the brakes. Companies need to reflect on how they treat their people. It's not profits OR people. As good leaders know, businesses don't have to choose one or the other.

You want your employees to be present, sell more, get more done and knock goals out of the park, right? If that's the case, doesn't it make sense to take time and invest in your employees? What would it look like if your employees came to work happier and healthier? Do you think they would give more of themselves? Do you think their performance would increase?

How your employees show up is a direct reflection of leadership at your organization. Many people are taught to take emotion out of business – to get to the facts and drill everything down to numbers. But it's not that simple.

The goal is to create a win-win for all parties involved. It takes collaboration, honesty, and transparency. It also takes us stripping off our robot masks and being more empathetic and human.

Let's take a moment and look at things from your employees' perspective.

Working 9 to 5: Jaded or Optimistic?

"9 to 5" written and performed by Dolly Parton. Do you remember the title song from the 1980 movie with Jane Fonda, Lily Tomlin, and Dolly Parton?[1] Perhaps if you watched it today, you would find it over the top or cheesy. Or maybe get some new ideas on how to deal with your boss. (I'm kidding, of course!)

The interesting fact, though, is that both the movie and the song illustrate some of the issues Corporate America still faces today. The lyrics reflect the mindset many employees have when they go to work each day. These thoughts stress them out, which means they aren't focused or productive. When that's the case, it impacts all aspects of your organization – especially your bottom line.

Let's break down portions of this fun and entertaining song so you can see things from your employees' point-of-view. Once you see where they are coming from, you can use that understanding as a base to build your strategy. You can minimize – and hopefully avoid – these issues all together by creating a culture that is grounded in true wellness.

> *Tumble outta of bed*
> *And stumble to the kitchen*
> *Pour myself a cup of ambition*

Have you ever done this at some point in your career? You wake up and you need to slam back coffee or your favorite caffeine-filled beverage just to get the motivation to drag yourself out the door so you can make it into work? This happens every day as employees lose their motivation and passion for their jobs. They clock in and

---

[1] Parton, Dolly. "9 to 5" 9 to 5 and Odd Jobs. RCA Studios (Gregg Perry), 1980. Album).

out so that they can collect a paycheck and pay the bills. That makes for a less than inspiring office environment.

> *Workin' 9 to 5*
> *What a way to make a livin'*
> *Barely gettin' by*
> *It's all takin' and no givin'*
> *They just use your mind*
> *And they never give you credit*
> *It's enough to drive you*
> *Crazy if you let it.*

According to a study done by Payscale, about 73% of managers and executives say that employees at their companies are "paid fairly," meaning competitively with the marketplace.... Yet barely more than one in three (36%) of employees at the same companies agree that they're paid what they're worth[2].

Yikes! That is a big disconnect. It is no secret that employees feel underpaid. It is one of the top three reasons why people switch jobs. Is a pay increase the only way to acknowledge and recognize your employees? I don't believe so. If you can't afford to give everyone a raise, the question then becomes: how else can you show your employees that they are appreciated and valued? Don't worry, I have some ideas for you in this book!

> *They let you dream*
> *Just to watch 'em shatter*
> *You're just a step*
> *On the boss-man's ladder*
> *But you got dreams he'll never take away*

---

[2] Anne Fisher, "Think Your Employees Are Paid Fairly? Most of Them Disagree", Fortune, March 11, 2016.
http://fortune.com/2016/03/01/employee-pay-salaries-fair/

On the same boat
With a lotta your friends
Waitin' for the day
Your ship'll come in
And the tide's gonna turn
And it's all gonna roll your way.

I hope no one experiences what these lyrics suggest! I do believe everyone's ship will come in, and bosses play a critical role in helping employees meet their career goals. But the fact remains, according to a Gallup poll mentioned in Forbes[3], that 50% of employees quit their job because of their direct manager. That's why I recommend training and development programs as a key component to every comprehensive and holistic corporate wellness strategy. Managers, especially those newly promoted, need guidance so they become more than just master delegators.

You may wonder why I include training and development programs as part of corporate wellness. On the surface, they may seem unrelated. In my opinion, however, corporate wellness is more than teaching employees how to exercise more and eat healthier food. It's about the health of your organization from the inside out – a missing ingredient in most corporate wellness programs today.

These lyrics, albeit extreme, reflect the mindset of some of your employees when they step through that office door each day. However, I believe that many common workplace issues are fixable – so there is hope!

---

[3] Jack Altman, "Don't Be Surprised When Your Employees Quit", Forbes, February 22, 2017.
https://www.forbes.com/sites/valleyvoices/2017/02/22/dont-be-surprised-when-your-employees-quit/#53c3ac0c325e

As a leader within your organization, your days are filled with non-stop emails, back-to-back meetings and putting out fires all day long. And a lunch break? Please! You probably order food to be delivered, or scarf down what you brought from home in between meetings (or even during a meeting) because you don't have thirty minutes to spare. That kind of down time is a luxury. Seriously, there are days where you don't even feel you have time for a bathroom break.

I use this song and these examples (even if extreme) to say that I can relate as both an employee and a manager, which helps me bring a unique perspective to the table.

A Little About Me

Before I dive into the key components of a successful corporate wellness strategy, I want to tell you a little bit about my background. My "career" kicked off at the bright young age of 13. That's when I had my first job at a local, family-owned jewelry store. (Don't worry, no child labor laws were violated.) I actually wanted to work! I guess, in some ways, I've always been curious about business.

I've always been proud of the work ethic my parents instilled in me at a young age. (Thanks, Mom and Dad.) That work ethic and my drive to succeed became especially apparent when I began my advertising and marketing career. I was determined to learn, grow, and show my value. I thought the best way to do that was by working long hours.

Those long hours added up over time, and eventually impacted my health. Not to mention, plenty of temptations lurked around every corner, such as candy bowls, pizza parties, free breakfast tacos, donuts, and even beer on Fridays! I loved the perks, and having the food around was a bonus – especially when I had back-to-back meetings, or an end-of-day deadline.

Looking back, I realize that I developed some bad habits. To put it mildly, I became a workaholic. The tendencies were always there; however, they really went into over-drive when my five-year relationship with my boyfriend ended. To avoid and cope, I worked. People seemed to be impressed with my dedication and how quickly I could deliver on projects, which only added more fuel to my fire. I placed more and more focus on my career and climbing that proverbial corporate ladder.

Then, in January 2006, I was in a bad car accident. Like so many sudden events, my health and my life took a complete turn. I dealt with a lot of back and neck pain. Nothings seemed to fix it, so I learned to deal with the pain. There came a point where my "power through" strategy – in both my professional and personal life – was no longer sustainable, no matter how hard I tried. After a while, my body screamed at me to slow down. I didn't listen.

A few years after the accident, the stress and the pain took such a toll that I took ten weeks of short-term disability to focus on my healing. I completely unplugged. I didn't check my work email. I went to physical therapy three times a week. I worked out and cooked healthy food. I went outside to soak up the Texas sun. I missed the people I worked with; however, to be free of the demands that come with advertising and marketing was a change I embraced.

When I returned to work, I quickly found myself swimming in the deep end of chronic pain and stress once again. I told myself, "Suck it up, Buttercup. This is life and I need to do what's necessary for my career." (Quite frankly, I counted my blessings that I had a great career and a job!)

I worked fifty to sixty hours a week, plus weekends. I didn't set up proper boundaries – and for that I take full ownership and responsibility. The truth is I used work as an excuse. (Remember, recovering workaholic over here.) I was stressed out all the time. It wasn't as easy to power through as it used to be. To be honest, I knew I worked too much. But I didn't think I had a real problem until I received a couple of wake-up calls that really grabbed my attention and shook me to my core – albeit almost ten years later.

The first wake-up call happened when I received a text from one of my best friends saying that a former boss and mentor passed away. I remember that I had back to back meetings that day, but I was in a complete daze. I went to my meetings and felt as if I was not fully in my body. My thoughts raced around. Tears came to my cheeks at random times during the day. My mentor's life was cut too short, and I saw similarities in the way we both approached work and life. I knew I was headed down the same road if I didn't change.

The second wake-up call happened two or three years later. At the age of 32, I woke up one morning with gripping, throbbing chest pains. I even had an odd sensation going down one arm. I thought I was having a heart attack. That experience scared me. I knew that the stress in my life was taking a toll on my health. After some soul searching, I figured out what I wanted: I wanted to start my own coaching/consulting business, because I didn't want my legacy to just be that "she worked hard."

I knew I had to make a change. It was not easy. At times, I felt alone in the whole journey. I discovered that, in order to create lasting change, you have to get to the root cause of what's going on. A surface-level solution, putting a band-aid on it, might help in the short-term. It might mask the symptoms for a little bit; however, the underlying issue will still be there. This truth applies to the corporate world as well.

Many of us feel the need to do everything on our own, as if admitting that we need help is a sign of weakness. I know I thought that for a long time. If I couldn't do something, it meant that I wasn't up to the task, or not good enough. Finally, I learned to look outside of myself and get help. That change made all the difference.

The same can be said about your corporate wellness strategy. You don't have to figure it out all on your own. You can get outside help. This book is meant to be a tool in your strategic toolbox that helps you see the value of corporate wellness, why it's important, and how you can implement strategies to avoid band-aid solutions that don't work.

We spend up to one-third of our lives at work, so companies need to understand that their culture, environment and leaders – critical and often overlooked components of corporate wellness – have an enormous impact on their employees' health and life. In my opinion, this needs to be taken more seriously. It is one reason why I'm so passionate about this topic.

My goal is to educate in a down-to-earth fashion so you can implement these best practices in your organization right away. I do not believe there is a one-size-fits-all answer. Each company is unique. That's why a corporate wellness strategy must be customized to your organization and its needs. That said, there are certain key strategies every company needs in order to create a corporate wellness program that delivers results.

Corporate wellness is a strategic response to low employee engagement, leadership, morale, productivity, and retention. It can also save you money on healthcare and talent acquisition costs, help avoid layoffs, and ultimately make your business more profitable.

Meanwhile, your employees will be happier and healthier. It's truly a win-win.

I believe companies need to prioritize their employees first. When they do, everything else follows. As Sir Richard Branson stated, "Clients do not come first. Employees come first. If you take care of your employees, they will take care of the clients."

Ultimately, this creates an opportunity for organizations and leaders, like you, to try something new and rise above the old-school, traditional approach to common workplace issues. Imagine for a moment, coming to work with employees who are excited, engaged, and passionate about giving you their best each day. When that happens, it will yield a more productive, profitable and thriving company.

CHAPTER 1
WHY CARE ABOUT CORPORATE WELLNESS?

Quite honestly, corporate wellness is a nebulous term that sometimes carries little weight in the business world. At the same time, it is a hot topic because everyone wants their employees to be happier and healthier so their productivity and profits go up.

But what does corporate wellness actually entail?

It's typically thought of as a program that includes Lunch n' Learns with local experts, nutrition advice via a boring newsletter, exercise or movement challenges, and healthy snacks around the office. It may include a gym discount and other benefits or perks. Corporate wellness is all of those things, but it is also much more.

It is a business strategy. Unfortunately, it's often not viewed this way. Instead, it's a very low priority for many organizations – the low man on the totem pole. It doesn't get the attention or time it deserves. It's an afterthought –

a task that someone checks off a to-do list so a company can publicly say they do corporate wellness. This mentality needs to change. When corporate wellness is done correctly, it can be the answer you've been searching for – one that addresses many of the challenges that can rot a company from the inside out.

It needs to be a business priority. At the end of the day, businesses need to control expenses. And let's face it, healthcare costs aren't going down any time soon. All companies want to save money on healthcare. They all want their employees to be happier and healthier. But who has time for corporate wellness? Most companies miss the fact that corporate wellness can also help improve productivity and increase the bottom line.

Some companies tried corporate wellness programs and didn't see results. Has this been your experience? If so, I get it. You aren't alone. There's a trick to all of it: Find the right strategy that works for your company. Doing what the company down the street does will not give you the results you are looking for, because each company is unique. The right strategy for your company will help you meet your corporate objectives while creating a culture where your employees actually thrive, so you see a return on your investment (ROI).

I believe corporate wellness is a strategic approach that addresses some of the common issues that plague HR and corporations around the world. Corporate wellness can positively impact and improve the following areas in your organization:

- career growth and opportunities
- internal systems
- cross generational management (i.e. working with millennials)

- business costs such as healthcare and talent acquisition
- conflict resolution
- employee engagement
- diversification
- health and safety
- leadership and management
- outsourcing
- negativity and morale
- productivity and time management
- recruitment
- reduction in sick days
- employee retention
- training and development
- work performance

Corporate wellness is more widely known as a feel-good luxury or a nice-to-have program instead of a business priority. But, when done correctly, corporate wellness can actually improve how an organization runs on a daily basis.

One comprehensive strategy can tackle all of these areas. Wouldn't that be nice? Do you feel lighter? Do you feel your shoulders relaxing? Hang on to that feeling as we dive through the key strategies you need to create a win-win for the bottom line and your employees.

Corporate wellness is becoming more of a hot topic because of the burn-out rate and stress employees experience every day. Companies are trying to be more proactive about adding corporate wellness into the mix. While I am overjoyed that corporate wellness is now more of a priority than it once was, most companies miss the boat when it comes to creating and executing an effective strategy.

For example, I had a strategy session with a financial organization that had difficulty engaging millennials. They wanted to lower healthcare costs and create a healthier environment for their employees, but their biggest need centered around retaining millennials. On the surface, it doesn't seem like this would be a corporate wellness issue.

After digging deeper, however, the strategy became clear: They needed to adjust their corporate wellness programs by creating more mentorship and leadership programs (a training and development issue). Investing in the employees brought opportunities for them to grow their career, which helped the retention problem.

Corporate wellness seems so counterintuitive. I like to think of it as an approach that gets to the root causes or issues within a company in order to create behavioral changes that yield positive benefits for the business and its employees.

So here's my question to you: What type of culture and organization do you have? Are you a traditional or established company that is stuck in the past because that's the way things have always been done? Are you a company that is open to making the needed changes in your organization so you don't have to lay off your people? Are you a progressive company that doesn't follow the crowd and is not satisfied with the status quo? Do you want to create a thriving culture and profitable business that will be around for years to come?

As Albert Einstein famously stated, "Insanity is doing the same thing over and over again expecting a different result." This mentality can be crippling to the growth and profitability of a company. It is time to do things differently.

For example, I spoke with an organization that, on the surface, wasn't seeking a corporate wellness program.

During our initial strategy session, they disclosed their biggest business challenge: Their sales team continued to use the same old tactics to win customers that they did ten to twenty years ago. They did not need healthy snacks, nutrition tips, or an exercise challenge to solve this problem. Instead, they needed to teach their sales team to evolve with the times instead of relying on old-school, out-of-date tactics.

First, they deserve kudos for the ability to retain employees for ten to twenty years. That's a huge accomplishment!

Second, believe it or not, this challenge can be addressed through implementing custom corporate wellness strategies. The sales team is doing things the only way they know how. However, customers today are savvier than ever, with the added convenience of technology at their fingertips. Businesses need to be authentic so that they rise above all the noise and stay competitive in the market. If you are stuck in old-school, traditional tactics you may see some success; however, to level up, you need to adapt and be open to new methods of reaching your goals. So what's the answer to this puzzle?

In this instance, the corporate wellness solution was all-around staff training and development – not just for the sales team, but for the managers as well. (Here's a bonus tip if you find yourself repeating a lot of the same tips over and over again in your one-on-one meetings. Find a way to record and store the training materials so that they can be reused again and again. This helps the issue on the sales floor and it's also a great tool to utilize when onboarding any new sales personnel in the future.)

As I said before, corporate wellness is more than a fruit bowl, a gym discount, or some awesome perks. That is the old-school mentality, and it does not typically get the win-

win results you want for your company. I have worked for companies where they tried to stop the bleeding with quick fixes. It's not pretty. It kills morale and productivity. It creates a breeding ground of negativity and distrust, especially between the executives and staff. There has to be trust and mutual respect.

Sometimes you have to take a step back and look at things from a different angle. Stop doing things the way they have always been done. If it's not working, then that means it's time to get a little more creative.

I believe corporate wellness is really about the health of your organization from the inside out. This new-school mentality around corporate wellness creates a company culture and a team that is healthy and strong. That's why I evaluate an organization across four key areas: leadership, physical environment, company culture, and employees.

So let me ask you, how does your company view corporate wellness? Are you in the old-school or the new-school camp?

There is no one-size-fits-all approach when it comes to corporate wellness. I do not believe in boring, run-of-the-mill, cookie-cutter programs, because they only get mediocre results at best. I work with companies that want customized, effective approaches to running their business.

My goal is for you to see corporate wellness in a different light – as a business necessity, the answer to many of the common workplace issues your company battles every day. It is an opportunity to bridge the gap between executive and employee relationships. It should be engrained in the day-to-day expressions of your company culture. I want to help companies create experiences that meet the needs of both the business and its employees, so it's truly a win-win for everyone.

I get Google alerts every day about companies laying off their employees. It's part of business, and there are always numerous reasons why a company resorts to that option. However, at the end of the day, it's all about controlling costs. If companies want to avoid or minimize the painful impact of layoffs, there must be a proactive strategy in place to do so.

One of the largest expenses a company has is with their payroll and benefits. Specifically, healthcare costs will only increase as time goes on. That's why companies must look at the numbers – the data – in order to create the best strategy for their organization. This is where so many companies miss the corporate wellness boat. They bring in a few health coaches, do health risk assessments, and maybe even have fitness classes or massage therapists come in occasionally, but then wonder why they don't see any positive returns. They don't see a decline in costs and they don't see many changes in their employees' behavior. It's because they are guessing!

Coming from the marketing world and having to show a positive return for every penny spent, I can't in good conscience create a customized corporate wellness strategy that is not based in data. If you want to say you are doing corporate wellness for the sake of it – because every other company is jumping on the band wagon – then that's cool; however, this book may not be for you. It cannot be something you just check off your to-do list.

Imagine what your company could really accomplish if you created a corporate culture with wellness at the center – a culture where the health of your organization from the inside out was the priority. Recruitment would be easier because your company would be seen as a thought leader. Employees would stay longer and not leave you for the competition, because they would feel like they are a part of something bigger than themselves.

They would feel appreciated, heard and valued. Productivity and sales would be up because your employees would be happier and more engaged, giving you their best every single day. The communication gap between executives and staff would greatly improve and the atmosphere of the office would be exciting and fun, sparking new levels of inspiration.

That's what I mean by a win-win solution – a program where both the business and the employees benefit.

The benefits of corporate wellness from the employer's standpoint include:

- lower health care and disability costs
- lower talent acquisition costs
- decreased rates of illness and injuries
- reduced number of employee sick days
- lower turn-over and retention rates
- increased employee productivity
- improved corporate image, reputation and PR
- improved employee morale
- increased commitment to and creation of a culture of health
- improved communication with staff
- less workplace conflict and drama

The benefits of corporate wellness from an employee's perspective include:

- increased well-being and self-esteem
- improved stress management skills
- improved nutrition, physical activity and lifestyle habits
- improved health status and energy levels

- lower out-of-pocket costs for health care services (e.g. – reduced premiums, deductibles, co-payments)
- increased access to health resources and social support
- improved job satisfaction
- improved work-life balance and personal life
- improved communication with management
- safer and more supportive work environment

Which of these benefits do you want for your organization? If your company is open and ready for change, if you want new strategies that go beyond the status quo, then let's roll up our sleeves and get this party started!

CHAPTER 2
HOW DOES A COMPANY'S CULTURE RELATE TO CORPORATE WELLNESS?

In theory, corporate wellness and your company's culture should be one and the same. The two concepts are tied at the hip. They are simpatico. They work together. Effective corporate wellness comes out of a company that has a positive and thriving culture. But how, exactly, do you connect the dots between corporate culture and wellness?

A company's mission, purpose, goals, and values work together in the creation of a company culture. These can be very nebulous concepts, so defining them is important so that employees can see how they should be manifested in their day-to-day operations. Weave those concepts and beliefs into your physical environment, processes, internal and external interactions, etc. If someone from the outside looks into your organization, they should easily understand what your company stands for and get a sense of your culture. It's not enough to state your culture in an employee handbook. The organization, leaders, and employees need to embody it and put it into action.

Corporate wellness complements corporate culture. Corporate wellness is not only about healthy snacks, gym discounts, weight loss challenges, etc. It's about the health of your organization from the inside out, which is why they intertwine and overlap. Basically, corporate wellness should be engrained into the fundamentals of your organization.

One of the reasons I am so passionate about corporate wellness is because I believe that the current system is broken. I've worked at a lot of great companies, but the reality is no company is or will ever be perfect. There will be growing pains, unhappy coworkers, bosses that frustrate their team, and decisions that some people will not agree with. And that's okay. We aren't striving for the "perfect place to work" because that doesn't exist. Most people work to pay the bills; however, I believe deep down that most people also want to work for a company where they can connect with good people doing good things for a good purpose.

But it is difficult for employees to meet that desire, especially if the organization itself is in chaos, if the leaders do not agree with one another, if the company changes direction every few months, if management offers more negative comments than words of positive encouragement, or if departments do not communicate with each other.

Working in these conditions breeds a whole host of problems. Everyone is stressed. Morale is on edge. Meetings seem pointless when no one agrees. At some point, your employees must decide if staying in that type of an environment is worth it, or if they should move on. I know I've stayed at organizations longer than I wanted to because I believed that the boat could be turned around and because I loved working with the team.

Your company's culture is 100% tied to its people. Your employees are the heart of your organization. If you take care of your employees, they will be dedicated and loyal, giving you their best. They will go above and beyond. They will take care of your customers, which benefits the bottom line. That is why corporate wellness can help with so many of the standard business and HR-related issues that companies experience day in and day out.

It seems counterintuitive that corporate wellness can help eliminate or minimize issues like morale, productivity, profitability, recruitment, retention, training and development, etc. The positive difference corporate wellness can have on your bottom line by saving you money on healthcare and talent acquisition costs could tremendously help a company, especially in a day and age where layoffs are happening every day. With these issues, executives don't always make the connection that corporate wellness could be the answer they have been searching for. That limiting perspective needs to change.

The goal of corporate wellness is to create a win-win strategy for all parties involved. An effective program will improve the bottom line and potentially any other business challenges you face, while at the same time creating a happier and healthier workforce. It will help your company avoid scenarios where your employees burn out and leave you for the competition because they don't feel supported. Remember, actions always speak louder than words.

Here's how you can make corporate wellness a key component of your culture:

- Prioritize wellness through your words and actions, from the top of your organization down. Ingrain the concept in external and internal communications. Show the habit in the ways managers interact with their teams.
- Provide easy access to information that helps your employees make better health decisions. Supply filtered or bottled water, healthy snacks, ergonomic desk options, gym subsidies, 5k walks for charity, team sports, etc. (Remember, these are examples of tactics that you can implement within your organization to prioritize wellness. This is not the actual strategy itself.)
- Encourage participation! Who doesn't want to live a longer, happier, healthier life to be around for family, children, grandchildren and friends? It's important to have a support system. That's why we build ways to include your employees' family members into your corporate wellness program. This can be done through incentives, health fairs, education talks, and more.
- Create an environment of learning and accountability. We should never stop being a student of life. Develop staff training and development programs, along with fun ways to hold each other accountable. As John F. Kennedy once stated, "a rising tide lifts all boats."

If you boil it all down, the Golden Rule applies here: Treat your employees like you want to be treated. Everyone wants to be appreciated and valued. Done well, corporate wellness programs show your employees that they are indispensable – an attitude which goes a long way in building a rock-solid culture. It may even get you on those Best Places to Work lists (if that's your goal).

Corporate Wellness Is A Two-Way Street

When it comes to corporate wellness programs, there is both a corporate and individual level of responsibility. Corporate wellness is a two-way street where both the company and employees have a role to play. It takes two parties to make a great culture – leaders as well as employees. How does individual responsibility play a role in corporate wellness? How can we bridge the gap between corporate and individual responsibility when it comes to your corporate wellness programs?

You can lead a horse to water, as they say, but you can't make him drink. As an organization, you cannot force people to implement healthy habits or change their behaviors if they do not want to do it for themselves. For example, you might bring in an expert to do a Lunch n' Learn on nutrition; however, if they decide to not implement that expert's advice, then that's their personal choice. This is where individual responsibility comes into play. Employees have a responsibility for their own health, life and general well-being. That isn't your responsibility.

You can, however, create systems that encourage individual participation. Dr. Gail Matthews, a psychology professor at Dominican University in California, conducted a study on goal-setting with over 250 participants. The study showed that people are forty-two percent more likely to achieve their goals when they write them down[4]. As part of your corporate wellness program, you can encourage your employees to utilize tools such as journals to track goals and activity in the areas of food intake, exercise, life goals, dreams, etc.

---

[4] Peter Economy, "This Is the Way You Need to Write Down Your Goals for Faster Success", Inc, February 28, 2018.
https://www.inc.com/peter-economy/this-is-way-you-need-to-write-down-your-goals-for-faster-success.html

You can also leverage technology (like mobile apps) to help your employees manage their time, water intake, exercise, or even provide healthy meal ideas and recipes.

If your employees are happy and healthy they will be more productive. You will retain your top all-star employees, increase morale, and lower your healthcare costs. Your responsibility as a company is to encourage your employees to live a healthy lifestyle through incentives, marketing, programs, and tools like those mentioned above.

CHAPTER 3
WHAT FOUR STRATEGIES ARE NEEDED FOR CORPORATE WELLNESS?

I began this book with the claim that most corporate wellness programs don't work. I believe they don't work because they are not strategic, but rather, more of an afterthought. I believe most are based on assumptions and not data. I believe most companies do not know how to measure or track the success of their programs. I believe that most corporate wellness programs do not have 100% support from all their leaders, and that they are not a critical piece of the company's culture.

Every company I work with, no matter their size, is at a different place in their corporate wellness journey. Each company has its own unique goals, needs, and objectives. Some companies "did corporate wellness" in the past, and it didn't work. Some currently have a wellness program, and are looking to improve their results or get new ideas. And some companies are starting from scratch.

Regardless of your company's experience, every successful corporate wellness program must include four key strategies:

- Define clear goals, objectives and desired outcomes.
- Conduct an honest evaluation of your company.
- Create and implement a strategy based on data.
- Track your programs so you know what's actually working.

Effective corporate wellness strategies also depend on your company's size. For example, if you implement the same corporate wellness strategies in your fifty-employee company that Google uses in their organization of over 98,000* employees, then you might not see the same results that they do[5]. The principles of corporate wellness still apply to your organization; however, the details and implementation strategies are different.

---

[5] Jillian D'Onfro, "Google Parent Alphabet Reports Surge In Spending And Hiring, Hitting Nearly 100,000 Employees", Forbes.com, February 04, 2109

https://www.forbes.com/sites/jilliandonfro/2019/02/04/google-parent-alphabet-reports-surge-in-spending-and-hiring-hitting-nearly-100000-employees/#22fbece772e8

CHAPTER 4
WHAT'S YOUR PURPOSE AND VISION? DEFINING COMMON SENSE GOALS AND OBJECTIVES

"Setting goals is the first step in turning the invisible into the visible."
~ Tony Robbins

As I mentioned before, my "9 to 5" job in the corporate world was creating advertising and marketing strategies for my clients. I helped them determine where to place their ads and how to spend their money so they could get the most bang for their buck.

In order to craft the best strategy for an effective campaign, I had to learn about their business – who they were, what they did, and what they wanted to focus on. I needed to know who they wanted to target with their ad, when they wanted to start the campaign, how much money they wanted to spend, results from similar campaigns they implemented in the past, and many other details. Most importantly, I needed to know their desired outcome. What were they looking to accomplish? What results did they want from the campaign?

Many factors determine whether an advertising and marketing campaign is successful, and the burden isn't placed on the shoulders of one person. In this instance, the client was responsible for making sure they provided all the necessary information. The creative team was responsible for the words and the visuals. I determined where to place the ad so the appropriate people saw it. Numerous moving parts and people were involved.

I want you to know that I get it. I understand how speaking in generalities is good in theory; however, I know that your company is unique. That's why I'm giving you this road map to create a custom strategy that works for your company.

Just like with an advertising campaign – or any business activity – creating goals and objectives for your corporate wellness program is essential. After all, without clear goals and objectives, how do you know where you are headed, let alone how to measure your progress?

The first step to creating your corporate wellness program is to understand your company's goals and objectives for the year and beyond. The wellness program's goals should align with your company's overall goals and objectives for the year. Most companies have goals relating to customer acquisition, hiring, and revenue, to name a few. Keep them in mind throughout this process.

Corporate wellness should not be guesswork, and it is not a cookie-cutter program. It's not like computer software, where pretty much every company uses some version of Excel, Word or PowerPoint. That's not what we want to do with corporate wellness. We don't want to use the same software as everyone else. Corporate wellness isn't a one-size-fits-all solution.

As I've said, the strategy that will work for your company may not be the same as the company down the street. If you have fifty employees and try to implement the same corporate wellness strategies that Google has at their organization of over 98,000 employees, then you might not see the same results. The principles of corporate wellness still apply to your organization; however, the details and how it's implemented change.

The need for a customized strategy becomes clear when you tie your corporate wellness strategy to your company's goals and objectives. Since each company's goals are unique to their business, employees, industry, and marketplace, their wellness program should be unique as well. Remember, there is no one-size-fits-all solution. Think about what will work best with your organization as it exists today. As this program – and your company – evolves, you can always change and create new goals!

Separate your goals into short-term and long-term goals. For example, your ultimate long-term goal may be to lower health insurance costs for your organization, since on average, 50% of company profits typically go to heath care costs. This is a great long-term goal. Think about what your company can do with the money you save! As you may have guessed, these long-term goals take time.

For that reason, it's important to create short term goals for your corporate wellness program as well. Think back to the list of benefits you identified earlier, such as increasing morale, increasing employee retention rates, reducing absenteeism, and increasing participation. These are great examples of short-term goals.

To make your goals actionable, I highly recommend making them SMART – Specific, Measurable, Attainable, Realistic, and Timely. This classic method forces you to think beyond a generic outcome and focus on the details of how you want this result to happen, and by when. It makes goals clearer and more defined, which minimizes confusion and questions down the road.

Below are high-level examples of goals you can create using this approach for your corporate wellness program:

- Lower healthcare costs by 20% by December of the current year.
- Roll out new corporate wellness program to employees by March of next year.
- Hold first annual vendor health fair for all employees and their families in June of next year.
- Increase participation in corporate wellness program by 30% by the end of this fiscal year.

Depending on your organization's size and your role within the company, you may have the option of creating your corporate wellness goals by yourself or with a corporate wellness committee. Regardless of how many people are involved in the creation of your goals, you need to set some time aside to think through this step clearly. Your goals will dictate your strategy, your tactics, and the results of your programs.

Remember to be flexible. You may need to adjust your plans or strategy as the needs of your company and employees change over time. That's okay! As John Maxwell pointed out, "Failed plans should not be interpreted as a failed vision. Visions don't change, they are only refined. Plans rarely stay the same and are scrapped or adjusted as needed. Be stubborn about the vision, but flexible with your plan."

Action Step:

Want me to review your goals? Let's set-up a strategy session to discuss. Go to: www.SpeakWithAlison.com

CHAPTER 5
A BRUTALLY HONEST ASSESSMENT OF YOUR COMPANY

"True genius resides in the capacity for evaluation of uncertain, hazardous, and conflicting information."
~ Winston Churchill

Once you know your goals, it's time to evaluate your organization – a process I call the Reality Check. When I work with a new client, I help them evaluate what they've done in the past as well as their current programs. We then create the best short- and long-term strategies that get results.

Proceeding without a Reality Check is kind of like buying toothpaste at the grocery store, only to find out you had two of them at home already. You forgot to take stock of what you already had before you made the purchase. Before you can create a new (or change an existing) corporate wellness strategy, you need to start at the very beginning and conduct an evaluation.

The purpose of an evaluation process is to bring awareness to what's going on in your organization, so you can get to the root cause of any issues. Stop pretending that everything is great if it's not. If you can't be honest about the current state of your organization, then you shoot yourself in the foot before you even start. But if you are honest and dig deep, you can create a win-win strategy that will benefit your bottom line and your employees. It will create true and lasting changes that will pay off dividends for years to come. If you want to lower your healthcare costs, retain your best employees, stay competitive when recruiting top talent, increase employee engagement and productivity so that you can boost your profits, a Reality Check is essential.

The question then becomes: What exactly do we evaluate?

When evaluating your organization (whether you already have an existing program or you are starting from scratch), you need to look at seven different aspects of your business: benefits and perks, company culture, employee engagement, employee sentiment, leadership, office environment, and history. Let's look at each of these areas in more depth.

1. Benefits and Perks.

What are those little extras that you do for your employees, beyond the traditional 401k and standard healthcare benefits? Do you offer them free bottled water, soda, or food? (Some companies have fun with this and do things like Free Beer Friday, Free Taco Tuesday, or donuts and fruit on Wednesday.) Do you offer a Summer Friday program where you give employees a certain number of days throughout the summer where they can take Friday off to have a long 3-day weekend? Do you have relationships with retailers that give their employees discounts on particular products or services, such as gym memberships, cell phone service, or a particular brand of laptop? All these little extra perks count. Write them down.

Next, think about how you communicate these benefits and perks to your employees, and how often. Your internal messaging and marketing strategy to employees is just as important as your external marketing strategy to customers and prospects. It is another piece of a successful corporate wellness program. If your employees don't have regular reminders, they will forget.

Most companies usually communicate their benefits and perks through an employee handbook, and emails they send out a few times a year. Employee handbooks (both printed or online) are usually boring, unimaginative and wasteful. And if you are really honest with yourself, the likelihood that your employees saw all of those hidden gems buried deeply within that employee handbook of yours is slim to none.

Here's the deal: I know you want your employees to take advantage of the perks you created for them, right? Of course, you do! Otherwise you wouldn't have them in the first place.

Think about it this way: On average, a consumer must see an advertisement seven to fourteen times before they can recall the brand or take action on it. The same premise holds for your employees – your "internal customers." These benefits and perks must stay front and center in their minds through frequent communication and in a variety of ways.

That communication doesn't have to fall solely on the shoulders of your Human Resources department. If you have a marketing department within your organization, I recommend that you leverage their expertise for your internal communications. Ask them for fun and creative ways to bring your communication and ideas to life. Allow them to think outside that proverbial box so the excitement spreads like wildfire.

If you don't have an in-house marketing team, consider hiring a virtual assistant or contractor for the task.

Action Step:

Evaluate your current communication frequency and methods, and test fun, new ways to bring your benefits and perks to life. Set up a meeting with your marketing team (if you have one) to brainstorm ideas collectively.

2. Company Culture

I worked for several companies who said their culture was one thing, when the reality was quite different (and not in a positive way). It can happen to the best of companies, especially when there are frequent changes in leadership or the overall direction of the company. When this happens, it can greatly impact the employees' productivity as well as their morale –both of which greatly undermine your company's culture.

As a leader, you need to mitigate the potential negative effects that major changes can have on the employees and the organization as a whole. Obviously, every company experiences growing pains and other issues; however, the way these challenges are communicated and handled makes all the difference to your employees.

Let's look at the seven most common mistakes I see organizations make when it comes to corporate culture.

1. Lack of clarity. If your leaders cannot get on the same page, you cannot expect the rest of your organization to follow. The first step is to get clear on your culture, mission and vision. A great question to start off with is, how do you want your organization to be remembered?

2. Keeping your culture "old school" and stagnant. Your organization's culture should not stay the same as when your company first started. It should evolve over time as your business, employees, and industry grow. With the evolution of technology, people are plugged in 24/7. Whenever possible, the typical 9am-5pm structure should be eased up, allowing for flexibility in schedules (which we see more of today). I understand that some industries must be stricter than others, but the point is to allow some wiggle room for people to meet their individual needs and to express their personalities within the company. This applies to things like dress codes, policies about decorating their desks, and flexibility with when/where they get their work done.

3. Not rewarding positive behavior. If your organization does not have a recognition or rewards program, then implement one ASAP! Reinforce the positive behavior of those people who live out the company's values every day and meet their individual goals. When employees see their coworkers get kudos, they will step up their game to emulate that behavior. A recognition program can be as formal or informal as you would like it to be. Managers should encourage their team members on a regular basis. It's so easy to focus on lackluster results or poor behavior; however, being encouraging and positive goes a long way in creating a culture and environment where employees actually look forward to coming to work.

4. Making assumptions. Get the facts and don't make assumptions. Making assumptions is like a natural disaster. Once you make assumptions and lead from that place, chaos can happen in an instant, without warning, and can cause permanent damage. Leaders should check in with their employees regarding how they feel about the company, the culture, and the organization as a whole. If you want to create a successful business and an influential culture, you have to get feedback from those that are on the front lines living and breathing those company values each day.

5. "Do as I say, not as I do" mentality. Executives and managers must practice what they preach. If you want your organization to have a certain culture then the leadership team needs to not just tell people what's important; they also need to show it in their actions. Your employees will not take you seriously if you say one thing and do another (a truth which extends well beyond the subject of corporate culture and leadership).

6. Lack of communication. It's one thing to talk about your mission, purpose, goals, and culture once a year, or to have those ideas written on a few pages within your employee handbook. It's an entirely different ball game when there is more frequent communication, including visual reminders throughout the physical environment. Remember, it takes roughly seven to fourteen times for a person to act on an advertisement that they see or hear. If you want your employees to integrate your culture, goals, etc. into their day-to-day work lives, then make sure they hear about and see it regularly. This is where you can engage your marketing team again to create some fun ideas to use in your office – especially since most people are visual learners!

7. Not listening to feedback. Create a culture where honest feedback is encouraged. You don't want your employees to be fearful that their job may be in jeopardy if they speak up. At the end of the day, feedback is not an absolute. It is information, and you have a choice to do something with it or not. Asking for your employees' opinions creates a more open, honest, and transparent culture. It shows that you care about their opinion and that you are striving to make their environment a happy, productive, and successful workplace.

Employees want to believe in – and be excited about – the mission, values, goals, culture, etc. of the company they work for. All too often, however, they do not. Instead, many employees drag themselves into the office, drowning themselves in crazy amounts of caffeine to stay awake because they don't love what they do. They really just clock in and out to collect a paycheck.

The good news here is that there is nothing on this list that you can't recover from. You simply need to make a course correction and continue to move forward. No organization is perfect. As a leader, it is important to keep an open mind and, more importantly, an open heart. The heart of your organization is your employees. If you take care of them, everything else will fall into place.

Action Step:

Identify if and how your company makes any of the above mistakes. Brainstorm ways to course correct so you can create a positive and productive work environment for your employees.

3. Employee Engagement

In this category, we assess if your employees are focused, engaged, and motivated. Think about these questions:

Are your employees engaged with your company's mission and purpose? Is it clear? Do they know what it is?

If they were on the phone with one of your customers, can they clearly articulate the company's mission in one or two sentences?

Do your employees know the company's goals for the year? If they don't know, then you need to work with the rest of your leadership team on how to communicate this clearly and get them pumped up!

What about their own personal goals? Do they feel they have a way to grow their career?

Getting your employees engaged and excited is key! One way to do this is to listen (no really, actually listen) to your employees when they give feedback. Employees want to be seen, heard, and feel like they matter. They want to know they make a difference and that their role helps the company move forward. If they feel like there is a disconnect, they will not engage as fully with company programs.

Now, there are way too many factors involved in employee engagement to put them all in this book. The goal is to have you start thinking about engagement. What does it look like today, and where do you want to be in the future?

Action Step:

Set up a meeting with all of your managers. Ask your managers to get a pulse on how things are going within their department or team. Have them bring that information to the meeting to see if you can identify trends and discuss ways to improve. If you already do this – great. Ask yourself, if what you are doing is actually working. Tweak any processes as needed if you are not seeing results.

4. Employee Sentiment.

Employee sentiment relates closely to both the company culture and employee engagement. It is all related; however, each category requires you to ask a specific set of questions. When it comes to employee sentiment, you need to understand what your employees truly feel about the company and their personal role within the organization. Are your employees happy, or is morale low? Are they engaged? Are they productive? Are your employees leaving you for the competition? If so, what's the turn-over rate? Use the power of data and observation to answer these questions.

If you don't know the answers, don't sweat it. Instead, ask around. Use your eyes and ears on the street – aka your managers. Get their opinion, as they often have more communication with frontline employees.

Surveys are also a great way to gauge how your team feels, and a great way to create a successful corporate wellness program. If budget allows, use a platform that is 100% anonymous so your employees can safely share their true opinions without fear of consequences.

Action Step:

An annual or bi-annual survey is not enough to understand how your employees feel on a regular basis. Instead, survey your employees four or more times a year to gain more consistent insight into how your employees feel. Use a tool like Office Vibe for easy-to-administer, anonymous surveys.

5. Leadership

Leadership is the most important assessment category. It can make or break a company, which is why so many people want to avoid this topic. Being a leader is not an easy position. The weight of the company, customers, and employees rests on the shoulders of your leadership team.

What leader wants to second guess the decisions they've made? Who wants to take a long look in the mirror? The reality is, if you truly want to evaluate your organization and understand what is and is not working, then you must reflect on your company's leadership. It all starts with that man or woman in the mirror. (Thank you for the reminder, Michael Jackson!) That includes you and your role, as well as all other members of your executive team.

As a leader, your approach, attitude, and mindset directly impact the results of any corporate wellness program. If your leaders are not on board, then it will be obvious to your employees that corporate wellness is not something that they should take seriously, either. And if it is not taken seriously, then it will not be a priority across the organization. It won't get the necessary attention, budget, or time to do it right. As a leader, you must communicate with your words and actions that you are invested in the program.

Action Step:

Without too much analyzing and over-thinking, answer the following questions with the first thought that comes to mind:

Is there a disconnect between executives and employees? Are all of the executives and leaders engaged with your employees, or do they lock themselves in their offices? You must find ways to authentically connect with your employees.

Do you offer training and development for managers? You don't want them to just delegate endless to-do lists to their team. You want them to rise up and become true leaders. As we all know, this type of leadership doesn't happen overnight, or just because someone gets promoted.

How is constructive feedback about the company and leaders received? Your employees need to know that they are safe to provide their honest opinions. After all, they are coming from a good place, right? They, too, want to help the company succeed.

6. Office Environment

The office environment often gets overlooked in corporate wellness programs. It's more than just ergonomics! How is your office laid out? What's the vibe when someone steps through the door?

Have you ever walked into an office – whether for a meeting or a job interview – and immediately felt a sense of the overall company vibe? You could probably tell if it was overly formal or laid back, organized or overcrowded. It's all about perception!

Whether it's the visual design or the energy of the office, the overall environment plays a crucial role in the mood, productivity, and overall well-being of your company and employees. For example, switching from harsh fluorescent lights to natural light can make a big impact on absenteeism. Employees won't go home sick because their eyes got fatigued, causing a headache or a migraine. (Yes, this really is a thing.) Instead, they will be more present and productive.

Remember, we spend one-third of our lives at work so it's important to make the work space as inviting, comfortable, and productive as possible.

Action Step:

Brainstorm ways to change up your physical environment to make your employees' lives easier. Simple changes like using ergonomic equipment or changing the fluorescent lights can make a big impact. Even adding comfortable seating, fun chair pillows, aromatherapy or plants can breathe some life back into a drab environment.

7. History: What corporate wellness programs (if any) have you done in the past?

Assessing past corporate wellness programs requires you to get your hands dirty by digging up the past and reviewing data. Data is the core of decision-making when it comes to corporate wellness (that is, if you want to do it right). In order to track your programs, you need to have a firm grip on what programs you have implemented in the past and their results. This may have been "before your time," so you may need to do a little detective work and check around to see what (if anything) was done previously.

Did you try weight loss challenges? Were you satisfied with the participation rate? Did you swap unhealthy snacks for fresh fruit or healthier options? Did you bring in local experts to teach your staff about healthier living?

Write down what you did previously, which elements of each program worked, and which ones did not.

As we wrap up this chapter, I want to end with some best practices on how to approach the evaluation process (aka your Reality Check).

1. Get honest and real. No ego or rose-colored glasses allowed. Take off the mask where you pretend everything is perfect the way it is today. Don't settle for "good enough".

2. Be realistic when you do your company's evaluation. Do an honest assessment of your company's culture and what's happening in your environment TODAY (not what it will be in the future).

3. Find a quiet place where you won't be disturbed. It's important to think clearly. Don't do this exercise when you rushed, emotional, exhausted, prideful, or overly idealistic.

4. Survey your employees. If you find yourself guessing more than knowing, then it's time to do a survey. Employee surveys can be a delicate matter, but done right, they will reveal the good, the bad and the ugly. Check out an example at: www.virtualcorporatewellness.com/book-sample-survey

5. Verify you're reaching all employees. If you have multiple offices and/or remote employees, make sure to evaluate how this structure impacts your company's culture and overall performance.

You don't want Band-Aid, short-term fixes that will crumble. You are in this for the long haul, so you can stop stressing and get the results you want both for your bottom line and your employees! An honest assessment of the areas outlined above will give you the information you need to build the proper foundation of your corporate wellness strategy.

Action Step:

Do you need help with your employee surveys? Jump on a call with me and let's discuss how we can work together to get the data you need to create a corporate wellness strategy that will get results. Go here to get started: www.SpeakWithAlison.com

CHAPTER 6
CREATE AND IMPLEMENT A DATA-BASED STRATEGY

After creating your goals and doing your initial assessment, it's now time to build the customized framework of your corporate wellness strategy.

We live in a world where convenience is all around us. Not to mention, we can customize pretty much anything we want. We go to Starbucks and order whatever tall, grande, venti concoction we want. We can print logos, our favorite quotes, or photos on everything from t-shirts to shoes to coffee mugs.

We are used to living in a world where we can make substitutions, omissions, and trades so often that when we can't have something tailored to us, we get a little bent out of shape about it. If we can't have it our way, then we don't want it.

Customization is no stranger to the corporate world either. When I worked at my previous companies, my job responsibilities centered around developing a specific framework and a detailed plan to get the most bang for the buck with our advertising dollars and to reach our client's specific goals and objectives.

To accomplish this task, I had to understand my client's company, their background, and the detailed goals of each specific campaign. Next, I had to determine which type of programs would make the most sense. Should their ad be shown on TV? Should it be online? Should it be in a magazine or on the radio? I had to determine the best media outlet(s) to deliver their message. It could be one media outlet or several, depending on the purpose of the campaign, budget and their target audience. Once I had all the details that allowed me to create the framework, I could then start building a customized campaign for my client. No two campaigns were alike. They were all unique and customized.

When it comes to corporate wellness, companies get so busy servicing their customers, bending over backwards to give them have the best experience possible, that employees often come last. Don't get me wrong, customers are absolutely a priority; however, you should always go above and beyond for your employees because they are the ones who directly help your customers. If your employees are happy, your customers will be happy as well. One way to make your employees happy is to create a wellness strategy that incorporates their feedback so that you customize a program that works for them (as well as for you). That way, it is a win-win for all parties involved.

Follow this seven-step process of how to craft and customize your customized wellness strategy and program.

1. Create a corporate wellness committee.
2. Create and conduct an employee survey.
3. Evaluate your health insurance claims data and determine what health issues are driving up your healthcare costs.
4. Use all of the data to rank health issues in priority order so you can address within your program.
5. Analyze and review your budget.
6. Implement your program and ensure employee engagement.
7. Maximize employee participation with gamification.

Step 1: Create a Corporate Wellness Committee (Optional)

A corporate wellness committee is a huge asset that can aid in the success of your program. A committed team from all levels of your organization that "champion" the cause creates a recipe for success. Your wellness committee can discuss new ideas, ways to engage employees in order to maximize participation and much more. Plus, it's a great way to get people excited and involved from the very beginning.

Your organization may have the luxury of hiring a full-time person dedicated to the creation and execution of your corporate wellness program, or you may need to ask your HR team to add this to their plate. Either way, having a committee is not a requirement, but strongly encouraged.

When done right, a committee eases the workload of creating and managing a successful program that gets results. If the burden falls on the shoulders of one person then you could be missing out on unique ideas that could really benefit your company. More importantly, if only one person handles all aspects of the program from strategy to execution, that person is more likely to make assumptions, rather than use data and collaboration, at the center of the decision-making process.

If you create a wellness committee, keep the following points in mind.

Include members that represent all levels of your organization: executives, office managers, middle management and frontline employees. When all levels of your organization participate, it really shows your employees that you are behind this strategy 100%.

As a committee, assign or vote for someone to be the team lead. This person is responsible for scheduling meetings and holding everyone accountable for completing their action items.

The committee should meet on a regular basis – at least once a month. You may need to meet weekly during the initial planning process. After you implement the program, check in at least once month to discuss both your progress and any feedback collected from your employees.

I also recommend rotating your committee members so that you keep fresh ideas flowing and prevent people from getting burned out. You can ask for volunteers or hold a contest to fill the positions.

Every member of the committee should be in alignment with the importance of corporate wellness, as well as the purpose of the group and the outcomes you hope to achieve together. Review your goals, objectives, strategy, vision, and evaluation results with all members of the committee.

Additionally, the information you collect in the remaining steps will be discussed with your wellness committee. Remember that, while there are data to review, numbers to evaluate, and action items to complete, this step is meant to be a fun and creative way to maximize engagement and participation so that wellness remains at the center of your company's culture.

Helen Keller said it best: "Alone we can do so little; together we can do so much."

Step 2: Create and Conduct an Employee Survey

Start the data-collecting process by conducting a survey of your employees. Find out their preferences about the types of programs that interest them, the formats for receiving information, and which incentives will ensure maximum participation. If you don't get your employees' opinions from the very start, you cannot build a truly customized program that aligns with their desires.

After the survey is completed, share the results with your employees so they stay involved in the process.

To further help you in this process, here are some popular wellness categories to include as survey options:

- disease prevention (how to prevent diabetes, heart disease, etc.)
- medical self-care (first aid, when to take your child to the ER or doctor)
- fitness
- smoking cessation
- stress management
- alcohol and substance abuse
- back care/ergonomics
- nutrition education (cooking classes, how to make healthy choices when snacking or going out to eat)
- hypertension education
- mental health education
- weight control
- health screening
- financial wellness

- family planning/parenting (adoption, fertility, school selection, saving for college)

This list is to serve as a guideline of topics you can add to your survey; however, it is not extensive list of all your options. Remember to add a line for "other" so they can add their ideas. Your employees' responses will guide the priorities of your wellness program. For instance, if your employees ranked weight management at the bottom of the list, you do not want to start your program by bringing in a nutritionist.

Friendly warning: do not skip surveying your employees. If you do, you set yourself up for a program that is based on assumptions. Most likely, it will not deliver a positive ROI. A mistake like that may ultimately put the kibosh on any future programs – especially those that require money. (OK, I'll jump off my survey soapbox now).

And don't forget to grab your survey example at: www.virtualcorporatewellness.com/book-sample-survey

Step 3: Evaluate Your Health Insurance Claims Data

You need to get a firm grasp on the issues that impact your employee's health. This step, therefore, involves evaluating your health insurance claims data. It is one of the biggest tools in your arsenal that allows you to customize your wellness programs.

You, as an employer, however, can only access limited information. You can only see high-level data due to HIPAA and privacy laws. Insurance companies can only tell you so much. The work-around solution in this situation is hiring a consultant. They can get third-party access to all the data and provide an in-depth analysis.

When examining the claims data, you want them to look at a variety of data points: age, sex, employment status, total healthcare costs, use of preventative services, diagnostic codes, procedure codes, and location of service. While it may sound like a lot of data, it gives you an overall understanding of the health issues that cost your company the most money. You can then create programs to reduce and/or prevent these problems in the future. That's a win-win.

For example, if over 60% of your employee's smoke, then you probably want to develop an extensive smoking cessation program. If 50% of your employees have high cholesterol, then you might look at developing programs that address various contributing factors to high cholesterol: nutrition, exercise, stress, and sleep management.

Additionally, it's important to review all of the dependent information so you can identify the issues your employees face at home. Employees bring their work life home and their home life to work, which can greatly impact their daily performance. Knowing the issues your employees face with their family members can help you create programs that will also benefit their families. You will also have more participation in your programs if you include your employee's family in the mix. Another win-win! (Side Note: If you cannot hire a consultant to review your healthcare claims data, be sure to ask your employees what health issues are most important to them in your employee survey. Adding more in-depth survey questions can be a work around for this step.)

Step 4: Use Your Data to Rank Issues in Priority Order

Once you have an overview of the health issues that cost you the most money, rank them in priority order to create a strategy. Brainstorm corporate wellness tactics to help eliminate and/or reduce the most important health issues first.

At this point, you have most of the data you need to understand the health issues and problems that your employees struggle with. You also have feedback straight from your employees about what they would like included in their corporate wellness program.

Using the survey results and claims data, brainstorm ideas with your committee. Outline what wellness activities will support your organization's long- and short-term goals, your employees' needs, and your program objectives. Don't overthink this. Start by listing fun ideas that you've heard your employees express interest in, such as adult sports leagues, healthier snacks, 5k walk/runs for charity, yoga classes, in-office visits from a massage therapist, etc.

Use big, wall-sized sticky notes to visually map out your ideas. You can even go offsite to a more casual location, so you can discuss ideas in a more creative and relaxed environment. It's always helpful to discuss ideas in a fun group setting.

After your brainstorming session, discuss and prioritize those activities and ideas based on the goals you created earlier in the process. It is important to pick and choose what activities make the most sense for the time being. Concentrate on doing a few activities well instead of trying to do everything on your list all at once.

To help you brainstorm activity and incentive ideas, download "150 Workplace Wellness Program Ideas That Get Results" at http://www.alisonbrehme.com/150Ideas

Step 5: Analyze and Review Your Budget

Once you choose which wellness activities to focus on first, analyze your budget. People often shift (awkwardly) in their seats – and sometimes even noticeably cringe –

when you talk about budgets, especially if you need to go ask someone (like your executives) for money to support your plans.

Here's the deal: I'm all about being efficient and effective with your dollars. I always view my client's budget as if it were my own money. With every marketing campaign I created, my goal was to get the most bang for the buck. I even created personal challenges to see how much money I could save my clients, which added fuel to my fire during negotiations. It was a fun game. How far could I stretch these dollars? So I would try to get the best price for every ad that we placed – no exceptions!

Being responsible for any budget is an honor, because not everyone is entrusted with this level of responsibility. I took it very personally. If we didn't get the outcome we needed, we constantly adjusted the program until we did.

I apply that same level of personalization, determination, and responsibility to my clients when we develop corporate wellness programs. I help you to be efficient and effective with every dollar you spend. You will not waste your money on cookie-cutter programs that aren't going to get results. You will not be spending money just to spend. You will not throw money down the drain! That is why I keep telling you to be very strategic with your corporate wellness approach and the wellness activities (tactics) that you chose to add to your customized plan. With that in mind, here are a few budgeting tips to consider as you build your wellness strategy and action plan.

The first step is to review your existing budget first and see what changes you can make before allocating more or asking for money right out the gate. When examining your budget, look at the miscellaneous spending across all departments. Find areas where you can cut back to make room for your wellness activities. Start with categories like drink and snack budgets, company-provided lunches, miscellaneous happy hours, etc. See how you can make healthy adjustments to your existing budget that align with the goals of your corporate wellness program.

Trust me, those on your leadership team will be grateful when you are proactive and suggest creative ways to leverage your current resources. Implementing a corporate wellness program doesn't mean you have to break the bank. Focus on how to redirect and/or adjust your current spending behaviors and purchases in ways that align with your goals.

Let's look at a practical example. Let's say you typically purchase water and soda for your employees. Now, with your corporate wellness program in place, you may choose to stop buying soda. You aim to decrease sugar intake and avoid the infamous 3 p.m. sugar crash (along with the irritability, lack of focus and mood swings that accompany it). Additionally, reducing sugar intake can help prevent the development of health conditions such as weight gain/obesity, diabetes, heart disease, tooth decay and cavities, and many other issues[6].

To meet these objectives, you continue buying the water and replace the soda with flavored sparkling water. You can make the switch all at once, or do a stair-step approach like I explain below (all with the same budget).

In the first month, you could purchase water, sparkling flavored water and sodas. The point in the first month is to introduce the sparkling flavored water while buying a lot less soda with the same amount of money. In the second month, you could purchase water, sparkling flavored water and caffeine-free sodas. By the third month, your employees will be somewhat adjusted – or

---

[6] Centers for Disease Control and Prevention, "Get the Facts: Sugar-Sweetened Beverages and Consumption", CDC, October 23, 2018.
https://www.cdc.gov/nutrition/data-statistics/sugar-sweetened-beverages-intake.html

make other arrangements to feed their habit – so all you need to buy is water and sparkling flavored water.

I recommend doing this stair-step approach with any major change, so your employees get used to it and understand the reasoning behind it.

Remember that you don't have to reinvent the wheel or spend large chunks of money to do a corporate wellness program. It's all about maximizing your current resources. Do what's best for your organization!

When you it comes to your budget, keep these things in mind:

- What can you do with the resources you already have?
- Be realistic with your company's financial resources and processes.
- Keep your goals and priorities in mind.
- Estimate costs for the activities you want to implement.
- Add a small buffer to your estimates (15-20%) to cover any unexpected costs that come up.
- Always negotiate with vendors to get the best price.
- Track your spending and make necessary adjustments.
- Adjust your current spending habits to make healthier choices that support your wellness initiatives.
- Be efficient!
- Do what's best for your organization.

Step 6: Implement Your Program and Ensure Employee Engagement

Now it's time to take the corporate wellness tactics that support your overall strategy and implement the committee's top picks. Regardless of your role, your corporate wellness program will only be effective when your employees care and participate.

You want them to be brand champions of your business, both internally and externally. You want them to join in when you have office potlucks, happy hours, events, or even a simple meeting. But often, it can feel like you are pulling teeth to get anyone to participate or volunteer. Enthusiasm might be high at first, but then they get busy or forget after the initial excitement wears off. To maintain high levels of participation, you need a strategy not only for the initial roll out of the program, but for ongoing communication as well.

How do you get your team to participate and stay engaged? That's what I want to dive into in this section so let's get the wheels turning! One of the most popular ways to get your team onboard is to include incentives. That's not surprising, right? Anytime there is a chance to win a prize (whether cash or non-cash), people are more likely to join in the fun. It's like buying lottery tickets or participating in an office football pool; there's a chance at the end to win something. Extra vacation days make a great non-cash incentive. Everyone loves a little extra time off!

While incentives are a great addition to any wellness program, they must be the "right" incentives that your employees will love. If it's not perceived as valuable, they may not care enough to participate. That will hurt your numbers. That's why I recommend that you include a question in your employee survey about what incentives would they want to see in a wellness program. Rather than making assumptions, do a little up-front detective work (a survey!) to find out what will motivate your employees to get onboard and stay involved.

While we are on the topic of surveys, I want to mention briefly (since we will get more into this in the following chapters) that when you roll-out a program, have an event, or host a guest speaker, I recommend that you do a couple of things. First, take attendance. (Flashbacks to grade school, anyone?) It can be as simple as a sign-in sheet. Understanding how many people participate in each event helps you track the success of your activities.

Second, as soon as that activity is completed, send a quick survey to your employees. Their immediate feedback will help you make improvements to the next wellness activity, so you get even better results.

Another way to elicit more involvement from your employees is to create team challenges, or hop on the gamification bandwagon (more on this below). This is a fun way to get employees engaged in a way that doesn't seem too boring or too structured. And let's face it: Everyone likes a little bit of competition every now and then.

You can create friendly competitions between departments and teams. You can do men vs. women or sales vs. marketing. Speaking from experience, trash talk may happen (okay it's pretty much guaranteed!), but it is all fun and games. You get the point though – it's a great way to get the excitement up and increase participation.

Also, keep the incentives simple and provide options. With corporate wellness, there is no one-size-fits-all solution when it comes to incentives. What motivates one person might not inspire another employee at all. Provide options.

Because we spend one-third of our lives at work, I encourage you to create a supportive atmosphere and a real "kumbaya," community feel. One way to do this is to include opportunities for employees to involve their family such as a health fair. As mentioned before, the lines between work and our home life these days are blurred. If you want to get your participation numbers up, make sure to include invitations to your employees' immediate families.

Last, but not least, include entertaining and frequent communication of your wellness activities. If you announce an event once in an email, chances are it's going to get overlooked or "accidentally-on-purpose" deleted. Most people are visual learners and need a little (or a lot) of reminders. Your employees have so much on their plates, they tend to forget things. Remind them often.

If you want your employees to be excited, you have to get a little creative. I know that's easier said than done. (If you're someone like me who can barely draw a stick figure, you may need a little help in this area.) Involve your in-house marketing team to help out. They might enjoy a nice break from the day-to-day routines where they can get let loose and ramp up the humor (maybe in a slightly irreverent but perfectly PC- and HR-friendly way). After all, it is internal communication, so have some fun with it! Whatever route you decide, the point is to make your communication come to life and to get your message in front of your employees more than once.

Overall, if you want to make sure your employees care, listen, and participate in your corporate wellness activities, involve them in the process by asking their opinion beforehand via a survey. Based on that feedback, you and your wellness committee can determine what approach and incentives work best for your organization. Ensure that people across all locations - and even remote employees – have the opportunity to join in the fun. Get creative, spread the word frequently, encourage friendly competition, and get excited!

> *"Instead of thinking outside of the box, get rid of the box."*
> *Deepak Chopra*

Step 7: Maximize Employee Participation with Gamification

You've implemented corporate wellness tactics and you've made sure people are participating. Now what? What can you do to take your program to the next level?

In today's technology-driven world, there is no shortage of apps that snag our attention, many of which are games. Games are enjoyable and fun. They keep us from taking things so seriously all the time. When games are used in various areas of business, it is referred to as gamification. Gamification is "the process of adding games or game-like elements to something (such as a task) so as to encourage participation."[7] Gamification is a growing trend in various industries like education and healthcare. Organizations like the U.S. Army, Jillian Michaels, Mint.com, and Samsung Nation are a just a few examples of companies who have implemented this growing trend.

A TalentLMS survey showed that 79% of the participants (both corporate learners and university students) said that they would be more productive and motivated if their learning environment was more like a game[8]. In this same survey, the results showed that:

---

[7] Merriam Webster, Gamification, 2010.
https://www.merriam-webster.com/dictionary/gamification
[8] Eleni Zoe, "The 2018 Gamification At Work Survey", Talent LMS, July 2018.
https://www.talentlms.com/blog/gamification-survey-results/

- 89% believe that a point system would boost their engagement.
- 82% are in favor of multiple difficulty levels and explorable content.
- 62% would be motivated to learn if leaderboards were involved and if they had the opportunity to compete with other colleagues.

We know that friendly competition can increase engagement, excitement, and participation. Gamification takes this to a whole new level. Adding a gamification component to your corporate wellness program can make the content "sticky" (such a sophisticated term) so they can remember and recall it later.

To gamify your corporate wellness program, you could choose a do-it-yourself (DIY) approach, or use software/tools to help make life easier. A DIY version might be as simple as having an internal website house your corporate wellness activities, presentations from expert Lunch n' Learns, recipes, etc. You could also have a scoreboard for those who attend events or visit the internal website, with the winners receiving incentives and prices. You could track all of this with unique tracking links for each individual employee so it's not all manual.

On the flip side, there are ready-made tools out there that can help you gamify corporate wellness and any of your other internal programs. For instance, visit https://technologyadvice.com/gamification/compare to see descriptions of various gamification programs, reviews and more. You can use the filters to narrow down the options which would make the most sense based on your organization's needs.

Gamification is not only for corporate wellness either. Think of the possibilities with this trend! You could use this approach when onboarding new hires. If you want someone to really understand your business from top to bottom, using fun tools like a quiz could help them retain the information. It would shorten their overall learning curve and make them more productive (which is always a bonus for the bottom line).

Gamification can be used for training and development, and even product education. This works great for teams which are the voice of your brand, such as sales and customer service. You want individuals on these types of external facing teams to know the ins and outs of all your products. Perception is everything, and if they can't speak intelligently about your products and services, then that hurts the bottom line. Gamifying your training sessions can go a long way to meeting your company's goals and making it more enjoyable for your employees at the same time. It's a win-win!

And let's face it: A tool that only helps with one area of your business is less likely to get purchased. On the flip side, if you have a tool that works for corporate wellness plus other areas of your business, you basically get more bang for your buck, and that request is more likely to get approved.

All in all, I would highly recommend including some sort of gamification component to your corporate wellness program. It may seem a bit overwhelming; however, it can be a powerful tool in your toolbox that can help you increase engagement with your employees. At the very least, I would stay on top of this growing trend so you can see how you can apply it in the future.

CHAPTER 7
TRACKING YOUR PROGRESS: SHOW ME THE NUMBERS

Now that you've created your corporate wellness program with tactics that support your strategy, you need to implement a process for tracking your program.

You have to track your wellness programs. This is not optional, especially if you want to reach your desired results and prove ROI. You can't ignore the data. You won't succeed in business today without looking at your numbers. There is no shortage of information to review on a daily, monthly, quarterly, and yearly basis. It is a necessary evil; the process of gathering and reviewing data can feel like pulling teeth.

I have a confession. Tracking is actually my least favorite part of this whole process. Even when I was in corporate marketing, this was my least favorite part. I love the strategy and building the action plans, but pulling and analyzing the data? Not so much. I worked on a team where one person loved spending his days buried in Excel data so much that we actually split up our roles. It was the best arrangement ever!

If you are one of those amazing people who geek out over the numbers, then this will be your favorite part. If you would rather go to the dentist than look at your data, then I recommend you delegate it if that's an option. Data is a critical piece of any business conversation, which now I have learned to love. However it gets accomplished, you must analyze the data because the numbers will help you make strategic decisions that get the results you want.

Where to Begin When It Comes to Tracking

When you start thinking about tracking, you will most likely wonder what metrics or key performance indicators (KPIs) should be tracked in order to prove ROI.

When you track your program, have your overall goals and objectives handy. This information will help you determine how to adjust your programs to ensure you get your desired results.

Also, in order to track any program, you need to create a baseline, or benchmark, for comparison purposes before you even start it. Ask yourself the following questions.

Have you done corporate wellness programs before? If so, what were the results? What does your recent health insurance claims data say? What are your current retention and turn-over rates? What have they been over the last 2-3 years?

These are great examples of a few data points you should know so you can identify trends in the numbers and track your progress.

Another reason it's important to track your wellness activity is to show what's working. Then you can continue those activities and allocate or request more budget as needed. No CEO, CFO, executive, or board will give you funds if you don't have a plan in place to show a return on investment (ROI).

Ultimately, the data you track depends on the types of wellness activities and tactics you plan to include, and how your organization is set up. Some common tracking metrics are:

- health insurance claims data
- health risk assessments (HRA)
- survey results
- retention vs. turnover rates
- participation
- absenteeism
- employee referral rates
- performance review scores
- award nominations
- vacation days
- timesheets

Let's dive into each of these a bit more.

Health Insurance Claims Data

We've discussed this a little bit already. Health insurance claims data is aggregated information of your employees and their dependents that provides an overview of their health and risks as a whole. This information is provided by your health insurance provider(s) and outlines what health issues have been impacting your employees and the associated costs.

Map your data to your long-term goals, which will most likely relate to lowering your healthcare costs. In what areas did you meet – and fall short of – your goals? Review the overall claims data over time to note if your employees have fewer claims, or if their health improved. In order words, do they benefit from your programs?

As I mentioned before, employers can typically see some aggregated data; however, if you want to dig deeper into the data you will need to hire a third-party consultant. There are ways to access the data without violating any HIPAA or privacy laws, which takes cooperation from all parties involved. Ultimately, the benefit is high-level intelligence and recommendations based on data so that you can create significant changes for you and your employees. If this information cannot be obtained, I recommend a more in-depth employee survey.

Health Risk Assessments

Also known as a Health Risk Appraisal, this assessment is typically a questionnaire or software that helps an individual determine the health of their current lifestyle. The results of this questionnaire are then discussed in a face-to-face consultation with a health advisor or via an online report that outlines the results and offers ideas on how to improve one's health and wellness.

Survey Results

After you complete a component of your program, get feedback right away! For example, if you do a series of three Lunch n' Learns with a nutrition expert, implement a follow-up survey to find out who signed up, who attended live, and how they thought the content/expert was (or was not) valuable. You can also see if attendance trailed off after the first session or stayed strong throughout all three sessions.

Retention vs. Turnover Rates

Most companies track this number and watch it closely. Evaluate if your employees stick around, and how that maps back to the average turnover rates you have seen historically. If you prioritize your people and they feel like their health and lives are supported both inside and outside of the office, then chances are they will want to stick around to make your organization a more profitable one.

Participation

Who showed up to your events? Was there a sign-in sheet, whether electronic or basic pen and paper? This can even extend beyond your corporate wellness program participation. Think about other areas where you want your employees to be engaged and participate such as training and development, volunteering, etc.

Absenteeism

How many people take sick days or "mental health" days? If you focus on your employees and prioritize wellness throughout your company's culture, they will likely use fewer sick days because they are taking better care of themselves. Of course, there are caveats to this generalization. For example, parents will take a sick day if their child is sick. Absenteeism is not a true representation of employee wellness; however, it's still a number to keep an eye on.

Employee Referral Rates

If your employees are truly happy, they will probably recommend your organization to other people. HR should be able to track this easily with the "How did you hear about us?" question on the application.

Many companies pay their employees a referral fee when they "refer a friend," so accounting may have a record of this information as well.

Performance Review Scores

Usually, when people are happier at work, they up their performance and productivity game, which can be seen in performance reviews and NPR scores. Look at the trends from one year to the next to see how individuals are progressing.

Award Nominations

Do you have internal employee awards? Do you ask employees to nominate or vote? If so, monitor the number of nominations. If your employees feel appreciated, supported and valued, they will probably want to participate more. This category also includes external award nominations for your organization. Did your company win an award or make the list for one of the Best Place to Work? Do your employees fill out those surveys and give you good reviews? Creating a culture of celebration and recognition is key to keeping employees happy.

Vacation Days

Do your employees take care of themselves and take the needed time off? A lot of times, when there is high stress or unspoken expectations, some employees feel they can't (or shouldn't) take vacations. They don't want to hinder their progress on the proverbial corporate ladder. Encouraging the use of vacation days helps you maintain a more happy, engaged, and productive workforce. Ultimately, it's important for your leaders to set the example.

Timesheets

Employee timesheets can be an excellent tool to determine not only productivity, but how much time they spend at work as well. Does an employee work the average forty to fifty hours a week, or do they consistently work fifty, sixty, or more hours a week? Train your managers to view timesheets as a way to assess the well-being of those they manage and help avoid employee burn out.

Define Your Key Metrics

Get clear on the metrics your organization wants to track before you begin so you avoid confusion down the road when you review your numbers. Understand that different sets of people within your organization will care about different metrics. For example, your executives may only care about survey results, retention rates and claims data to see if their healthcare costs are going down. On the flip side, HR or your wellness committee might want to look at more of the nitty-gritty details.

The point is to make sure you discuss and prioritize your metrics, and then consistently track them. It's also vitally important to track your current activity against historical data. If you don't have historical data, start tracking it now. If you do have historical data, utilize it as a benchmark for your progress moving forward.

You have to track results. This is not optional, as you have to prove ROI. Once you start collecting data, then you will need to report that up the chain so to speak. Discuss these numbers with your wellness committee on a regular basis as well.

The wellness activities you implement will dictate the type of information you track and how detailed. Just know that, with ANY program or tactic, there is always a way to track activity, even if you have to get a little creative. What your organization cares about may be different from another company down the street. Track and communicate the key metrics or KPIs that makes sense for your organization.

Optimizing Your Corporate Wellness Program

Now that you've determined what metrics to track, we need to talk about a process that most companies tend to skip in the execution of a corporate wellness program. You do not want to roll out a program and assume it's perfect from the start. You need to review the data and see how you can improve your programs and increase your outcomes through a process called Optimization.

Optimization is an important step in reaching the desired outcomes and ROI for your corporate wellness programs. This is why it's important to have more than one person working on your wellness strategy and its execution. Your job is not done once you launch your program, or even after you report the numbers to your executive team. You need to review the data and see how you can improve upon your programs to increase your ROI. This comes from listening to your employees (and the data). You can never simply "set it and forget it."

Here's an example of a mini-optimization process you can use in your organization:

1. Reference your benchmark and historical data. Regardless of what metrics you prioritize, you need to determine what your historical numbers have been (if any), so you can compare them against current and future data. This will help you to illustrate your program's progress over time.

2. Track the desired data and share the results with your wellness committee. Discuss what elements are working and what's not working. For the elements that are NOT working, brainstorm ways to adjust the program so that the participation, performance, etc. will increase.

For example, if you bring in an expert and your survey data indicates that the employees are happy with the presentation, you may choose to bring in that expert more frequently. Another course of action might be to find other similar experts for future presentations. On the flip side, if you see that a nutrition or healthy eating challenge has a low participation, then adjust it for better results, or skip it and do something else.

3. Brainstorm new ideas with your committee. This could include additional corporate wellness tactics that you want to implement. Once you have a list of those new ideas, I recommend creating another survey. (Yep, that's right - another one!) You need constant feedback to make sure your new ideas are on the right track. Always include an open-field question at the end of the survey questions to allow employees to provide their thoughts. It will make them feel like they are part of the process.

4. Gather the results from the survey. Then discuss those results (along with any recent claims data, depending on how much time has passed) with your committee again.

5. As a group, prioritize the top 3-5 ideas, pending budget and time. Create a revised action plan that adjusts your existing programs so that your results continue to improve.

6. Communicate to employees. Make the necessary adjustments, and then communicate them to your employees, emphasizing that you utilized their feedback to make this program better for them. Remember, as you roll out new programs, make them both engaging and fun!

Nothing that we create is perfect from the very start, so you have to optimize and adjust your program in order to reach your goals. If you commit to this process, it will help you increase engagement and retention rates and help you lower your healthcare costs. Remember, all companies are unique, so modify these recommendations based on what makes sense for your organization. Do what's best for you and your employees!

Tracking and optimizing your programs is paramount to your corporate wellness success. What you track, and how you approach and optimize the information will vary from organization to organization. These are ideas meant to help guide your conversations internally; however, are by no means an absolute – or even an exhaustive – list of ideas. The goal is to constantly improve your numbers and create a company culture where constant feedback is encouraged. If you do, your employees will feel like they are a crucial part of the process – which they are. But more importantly, they will feel even more connected and vested in your company and its future.

Analysis Paralysis

A word to the wise: When it comes to data, it is easy to get lost in the weeds. It's often referred to as analysis paralysis, where you overthink the data, causing indecisiveness and a lack of forward momentum. Basically, you talk about the data so much that you don't take any action. This can put you into a reactive mode instead of being proactive and strategic.

Get clarity around the data your executives need to review on regular basis in order to determine your corporate wellness program success. Get this feedback from them as early on in the process as possible.

Analyzing and reviewing data can become tedious and overwhelming. (Trust me, I am speaking from lots of experience in this area!) You can end up talking the numbers to death, providing rationale for the results and changing directions constantly without giving your strategy enough time to work. Do not do that!

Despite your best efforts, sometimes other factors (not present in the data itself) impact your results. For instance, if you create a corporate wellness program to improve retention rates and increase morale while trying to lower healthcare costs, but employees do not participate and there seems to be a mass exodus from the company, then other factors need to be addressed.

These outside factors will influence your numbers, so it's important that you don't give up on your program. Take a step back from the data and think about what other factors may be involved.

To investigate, you may ask yourself some questions such as:

Are there issues with managers or leadership? Is your compensation not competitive? Is there little or no flexibility with employee's schedules? These factors may not be represented in your numbers per se when you track your corporate wellness programs; however, they will influence your numbers.

Regardless, you need to report on your corporate wellness programs to show ROI. At the same time, you don't want to get so lost in the numbers that you lose focus on the overall goals, purpose, and mission. You need to find the right balance for your company. This step-by-step approach should position your company so that the numbers are in your favor. If not, ask your employees, get feedback and adjust!

Your Tracking and Optimization Action Steps:

- Know your goals.
- Have your baseline/benchmark data.
- Track everything, big or small.

- Aggregate the data and find the key trends.
- Create reports with executive summary, plus any relevant charts and data.
- Communicate results and progress to key stakeholders.
- Optimize and make any adjustments as needed.

Action Step:

Feeling overwhelmed by all the tracking and optimizing talk? It can be a huge undertaking! That's where consultants, like me, come in handy. Let's set up a complimentary strategy session to discuss your business needs further. Go to my calendar now: www.SpeakWithAlison.com

WRAP UP

"If everyone is moving forward together, then success takes care of itself."
~ Henry Ford

The goal of this book was to help you see corporate wellness in a new light. It's more than benefits or perks. It's more than healthy snacks or gym discounts. These are all great tactics, but it's not a strategy.

Your organization is unique. That's why these strategies and processes provide a customizable road map to guide you in creating a corporate wellness program that's right for your company, no matter its size. You will be golden if you create clear goals, make decisions based on data, have fun when implementing the program, and remember to adjust as you go so you can improve your results.

Remember, if you have fifty employees and try to implement the same corporate wellness strategies that Google has at their organization of over 98,000 employees, you might not see the same results. The principles of corporate wellness still apply to your organization; however, the details and how it's implemented change.

There is no one-size-fits all approach when it comes to corporate wellness, and I do not believe in boring-run-of-the-mill-cookie-cutter programs. They only get mediocre results at best, and your company deserves better than that.

Imagine what your company could accomplish if you created a corporate culture with wellness at the center – where the health of your organization from the inside out was the priority. Recruitment would be easier because your company would be seen as a thought leader. Employees would stay longer and not leave you for the competition because they feel like they are a part of something bigger than themselves. They would feel appreciated, heard, and valued. Productivity and sales would be up because your employees would be happier and more engaged, giving you their best every single day. The communication gap between executives and staff would greatly improve, and the atmosphere of the office would be exciting and fun, sparking new levels of innovation.

When it comes to corporate wellness, companies get so busy servicing their customers and bending over backwards to give them have the best experience possible, the employees often come last. It is important to create a culture of constant feedback so your employees are involved and invested in your organization and its future.

The lifeline of your company is your employees. If you take care of them, you create a win-win-win for you, your customers, and your employees. A customized, effective corporate wellness strategy can do exactly that.

Work with Me

If you have questions or need additional support, I support companies as a consultant, working alongside you and your team to create a solid corporate wellness program on an ongoing basis. I also train corporate HR teams so that they have the strategies and tools in place to implement programs successfully themselves. To get more information, go to: www.SpeakWithAlison.com so we can chat further.

ABOUT THE AUTHOR

Alison Brehme is a Certified Transformational Nutrition Coach who spent 15+ years in corporate advertising where she dealt with workaholism, chronic pain and saw how burnout and stress took a toll on her own health as well as the health of her colleagues. It was an eye-opening experience that led her to bring health and wellness back to the workplace as a Certified Corporate Wellness Consultant.

Virtual Corporate Wellness helps businesses retain and recruit top talent, increase employee productivity and become known as one of the best places to work. If you want to lower your company's healthcare and talent acquisition costs, close the communication gap between executives and staff, and create a culture where wellness is at the center creating a happier, healthier and more productive work environment then Alison can help.

She's been mentioned and published in USA Today, Fast Company, USA Weekly, Glassdoor.com, Corporate Wellness Magazine, Well.org and more.

Recently, she also created a brand called Let It Be Club (www.letitbe.club), which reminds strong high-achieving women how to slow down and become present to what matters most in their life so that they can make an even greater impact in this world.

Her main goal is to deliver high quality work and create positive results for her one-on-one and corporate clients.

RESOURCES

Below are important links mentioned within the book all in one place for reference.

Alison's Website:
https://virtualcorporatewellness.com

150 Corporate Wellness Ideas:
www.alisonbrehme.com/150Ideas

Sample Employee Survey:
www.virtualcorporatewellness.com/book-sample-survey

Book a Call:
www.SpeakWithAlison.com

Gamification Solutions:
https://technologyadvice.com/gamification/compare

Office Vibe[9] Survey Software:
www.officevibe.com/partner/virtualcorporatewellness.com

---

[9] Disclosure: I'm an affiliate partner with Office Vibe; however, I only recommend products that I have reviewed personally and meet high quality standards. This tool can make surveying easier so that you get micro-feedback on regular basis.

CPSIA information can be obtained
at www.ICGtesting.com
Printed in the USA
LVHW091104041119
636250LV00005B/1680/P